THE COVID-19 PANDEMIC:

The World Turned Upside Down

Hal Marcovitz

ReferencePoint
Press®

San Diego, CA

LIBRARY OF CONGRESS CATALOGING-IN-PUBLICATION DATA

Names: Marcovitz, Hal, author.
Title: The COVID-19 pandemic : the world turned upside down / by Hal
    Marcovitz.
Description: San Diego, CA : ReferencePoint Press, Inc., 2021. | Includes
    bibliographical references and index.
Identifiers: LCCN 2020022076 (print) | LCCN 2020022077 (ebook) | ISBN
    9781678200183 (library binding) | ISBN 9781678200190 (ebook)
Subjects: LCSH: COVID-19 (Disease)--Juvenile literature. |
    Epidemics--Juvenile literature.
Classification: LCC RA644.C67 M37 2021 (print) | LCC RA644.C67 (ebook) |
    DDC 616.2/41--dc23
LC record available at https://lccn.loc.gov/2020022076
LC ebook record available at https://lccn.loc.gov/2020022077

CONTENTS

A Danger to All

Dimitri Mitchell woke up early on the morning of March 21, 2020, feeling very ill. The senior at Clear Creek Amana High School in Tiffin, Iowa, suffered from a cough, fever, watery eyes, sweats, and a headache. "He came into my room and woke me up at 4 a.m.," recalls Mitchell's mother, Irene Yoder. "He was really sick with a cough and chills, so we went to the emergency room."[1]

Physicians at the local hospital diagnosed Mitchell with the flu and sent him home with instructions to stay in bed and take cough syrup. But over the next two days Mitchell's condition worsened. Most significantly, Mitchell developed a headache that he found virtually unbearable. "I was bedridden all day and I felt totally drained," he said. "My eyes wouldn't stop watering, I had the worst headache I've ever experienced and my cough was just getting worse and worse."[2]

It had occurred to both Mitchell and his mother that he could be suffering from an illness much worse than the flu. For weeks, the disease known as COVID-19 (caused by a new coronavirus) had been making its way across the world. By the time Mitchell woke up feeling ill, tens of thousands of people had been afflicted on nearly every continent. The first cases had been reported in America just three weeks before Yoder took her son to the emergency room.

By this time, the state of Iowa had established a hotline for Iowans to call if they had questions about

COVID-19. Yoder called the hotline and spoke with a state public health worker, who authorized a COVID-19 test for her son. A local hospital administered the test, and two days later the results were reported: Mitchell had contracted the disease.

Declared a Pandemic

COVID-19 is a highly contagious, potentially deadly disease. By the end of May 2020, according to a Johns Hopkins University tally, worldwide the virus had infected more than 8.7 million people and killed more than 460,000. The number of COVID-19 deaths in the United States had surpassed all other countries. By the end of May 2020, nearly 2.25 million people in the United States had contracted the virus and more than 119,000 people had died from the disease. Virtually every country on earth reported cases. For the better part of 2020, the disease caused entire countries to all but shut down. People were told to stay home and have no close contact with anyone outside their immediate households.

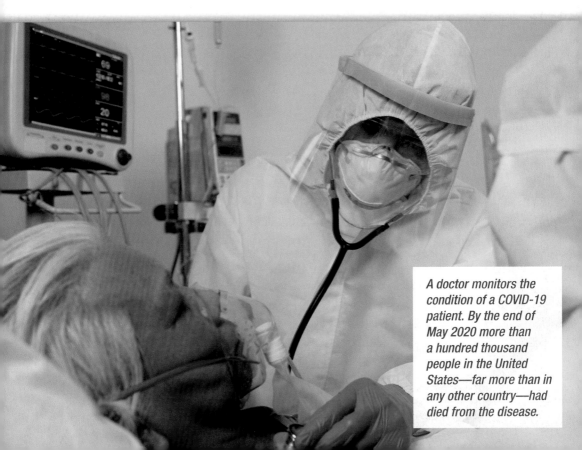

A doctor monitors the condition of a COVID-19 patient. By the end of May 2020 more than a hundred thousand people in the United States—far more than in any other country—had died from the disease.

And when they did venture out, for trips to grocery stores or pharmacies or for other vital purposes, they often fell under orders from their state governments to wear cloth masks. The masks were intended to prevent microscopic particles contained in their breath from coming into contact with other people—the primary method of spreading the disease.

On March 11, 2020, the World Health Organization (WHO), an agency of the United Nations that tracks international threats to public health, declared the spread of COVID-19 a pandemic. As defined by WHO, a pandemic is a disease that has spread across the world, afflicting large numbers of people. Eric Toner, a senior scientist at the Johns Hopkins Center for Health Security, an organization based in Baltimore, Maryland, that assesses worldwide health threats, applauded WHO's announcement. He commented that it should leave little doubt that COVID-19 represents a threat to the health and safety of people worldwide. "I am very glad they are making this announcement," Toner said. "To many of us, it has been a pandemic for several weeks. I think this removes any ambiguity about the global situation. This disease is spreading around the world. I think they are saying to all governments, 'You really need to get ready to implement measures to slow the spread within your own country.'"[3]

Affecting All Ages

After receiving his diagnosis for COVID-19, Mitchell was able to wait out the disease at home. Yet this is not an option for many patients who find themselves unable to breathe on their own. These patients have to be hospitalized and placed on ventilators, which are mechanical devices that propel air into their lungs. But since Mitchell was able to breathe without assistance, he did not need to be hospitalized.

Still, he experienced chills, coughing, and headaches during the two weeks he self-quarantined at home. "I was checking on him like every 10 minutes because I was scared," Yoder said. "He was so sick and weak and I was just making sure he was drinking lots of fluids and giving him cold compresses for his head, and when I wasn't watching him, I was cleaning everything."[4]

Eventually, Mitchell's fever broke. The sweats stopped. The coughing persisted for a few more weeks, although not as severely as when he was mired in the worst symptoms. Eventually, physicians declared that Mitchell had recovered from the virus.

Mitchell believes he contracted COVID-19 at a local grocery store where he worked part-time. In fact, when he was first diagnosed with COVID-19, he became one of more than eight hundred residents of Tiffin to have contracted the disease. Many of the people infected with COVID-19 in Tiffin—and elsewhere—are elderly. (As the disease spread across the United States, many state health departments reported that as many as half their reported deaths occurred in nursing homes.) These are people whose immune systems have been compromised by advanced age or other factors, such as previous diseases that have lessened their abilities to fight off infections. It means their bodies are less able to endure the symptoms. Still, the fact that an eighteen-year-old high school senior who was otherwise in perfect health could contract a life-threatening illness, perhaps from the breath of a grocery store shopper, illustrates how COVID-19 has posed a significant danger to everyone, regardless of age.

> "He was so sick and weak and I was just making sure he was drinking lots of fluids and giving him cold compresses for his head, and when I wasn't watching him, I was cleaning everything."[4]
>
> —Irene Yoder, the mother of eighteen-year-old COVID-19 patient Dimitri Mitchell

The Pandemic Spreads Across the Globe

Wet markets are common throughout Asia. They are places that feature dozens of stalls, where merchants sell meat, fish, and poultry, often slaughtering the animals right in their stalls. Journalist Jason Beaubien describes a wet market he visited in Hong Kong:

> It's quite obvious why the term "wet" is used. Live fish in open tubs splash water all over the floor. The countertops of the stalls are red with blood as fish are gutted and filleted right in front of the customers' eyes. Live turtles and crustaceans climb over each other in boxes. Melting ice adds to the slush on the floor. There's lots of water, blood, fish scales and chicken guts. Things are wet.[5]

Scientists have warned about the public health hazards of wet markets. Not only do merchants typically practice little hygiene in their stalls, but the animals—some wild, some domesticated—are often under stress while they are held in cages in these chaotic markets. These high stress levels can lower the animals' immune systems, creating environments where diseases from different species can intermingle—jumping from a chicken to a hog, for example. Soon, these diseases have the potential to become zoonotic—meaning they can transition from animals to people. According to Felicia Keesing, a professor of ecology at Bard College in Annandale-on-Hudson, New York, "If we needed to make a perfect recipe how to make a pathogen jump, that would be it."[6]

In late 2019, a disease is believed to have become zoonotic, jumping from either a bat or a pangolin—commonly known as a scaly anteater—to a person at a wet market in the Chinese city of Wuhan. Within weeks, COVID-19—the disease that emerged from the Wuhan wet market—was declared a worldwide pandemic.

> "If we needed to make a perfect recipe how to make a pathogen jump [from animals to humans, an Asian wet market] would be it."[6]
>
> —Felicia Keesing, a professor of ecology at Bard College in Annandale-on-Hudson, New York

The Disease Spread Quickly

Deadly pandemics have occurred before. In 1347, a plague known as the Black Death spread across Europe and beyond, killing some 137 million people worldwide. And in the two years following the end of World War I in 1918, the Spanish flu spread

Vendors await customers in a Hong Kong wet market. Scientists believe the new coronavirus, which caused the COVID-19 pandemic, emerged from a wet market in Wuhan, China.

from Europe to America and other countries, taking some 50 million lives worldwide.

But neither the Spanish flu nor the Black Death traveled with the swiftness of COVID-19. The speed with which the disease spread from China to other parts of Asia and on to Europe, North America, and other continents can be attributed largely to the availability of long-distance travel in the twenty-first century. In other words, a traveler infected with COVID-19, but not yet showing symptoms, could board a plane in China and arrive in the United States just hours later—perhaps infecting many people onboard as well as in the airports and elsewhere. And those peo-

How Viral Infections Affect People

COVID-19 is a disease caused by a viral infection. In this case, the virus is known as a coronavirus because when it is observed under a microscope, it resembles an orb surrounded by a hazy crown. The Latin word for "crown" is *corona*. The World Health Organization named the disease on February 11; *COVID-19* stands for "corona virus disease of 2019."

There are many different types of viruses and many different illnesses that result from viral infections. The common cold is a mild form of a viral infection, perhaps afflicting a patient with a sore throat, cough, runny nose, and slight fever for a few days. Or, as in COVID-19, a viral infection can prompt severe symptoms that can be fatal.

A virus is a germ. When a virus enters the body, it attaches itself to healthy cells, injecting its genetic material into those cells. That allows the virus to duplicate itself in the body. It also damages the cells, which, in turn, cause the patient to suffer symptoms such as headaches, fevers, and difficulty breathing. Many people have strong immune systems that help them either experience no symptoms from a virus or endure the infection with mild symptoms. Others, such as elderly people or those whose immune systems have been compromised by prior illnesses, may experience severe symptoms. Because of the harsh symptoms experienced by otherwise healthy people, COVID-19 is among the deadliest diseases to have been sparked by a virus in the history of human culture.

ple, in turn, could infect others. As Victor Davis Hanson, a history professor at Stanford University in California, explains, "Modern life squeezes millions into cities as never before. Jet travel, with its crowded planes and airports, can spread diseases from continent to continent in hours."[7]

The first reported death from COVID-19 occurred on January 11, when a sixty-one-year-old customer of the Wuhan market succumbed to the disease. The death occurred just before the lunar new year, which is a major holiday in China; millions of Chinese citizens travel to celebrate the holiday with family members in other cities. It is likely that many of those travelers unknowingly spread the disease to others throughout China and elsewhere.

On January 16, authorities in Japan disclosed that a Japanese man who had traveled to Wuhan was now infected with COVID-19. In the United States, the first case was confirmed on January 20 in the state of Washington. Cases also surfaced in South Korea, Taiwan, and Thailand. On January 23, Chinese authorities closed the city of Wuhan to travel and ordered all of its residents to stay in their homes. By this point, 17 people had died in China, and the number of infected people worldwide stood at 570. The first death outside China—a forty-four-year-old man in the Philippines—was reported on February 2. The death toll by that date stood at more than 200, with some 9,800 cases reported around the world.

The *Diamond Princess*

Some of those cases were found among the thirty-six hundred passengers aboard the *Diamond Princess* cruise ship, which docked in Yokohama, Japan, on February 5. The passenger list included more than four hundred Americans. The passengers were quarantined aboard the cruise ship, where the disease spread throughout the close quarters of the vessel. Screenings aboard the ship detected more than six hundred cases. On February 19, passengers who had tested negative for the disease were permitted to leave the ship and return to their homes.

In rapid succession, reports of the disease came from countries around the world. The first case in Europe was announced on February 14, when officials in France said an eighty-year-old tourist from China had died in a Paris hospital. It was the first known death from the disease outside Asia. On February 21, the disease surfaced in the Middle East when Iran reported the deaths of four COVID-19 patients. The African nation of Nigeria reported its first case on February 28. Two days earlier the disease had surfaced in Latin America. On February 26 Brazilian officials announced that a sixty-one-year-old man from São Paulo had tested positive after returning from a business trip to Italy. In fact, Italy as well as Spain were among the hardest-hit countries in Europe. By late April, Italy had reported more than 201,000 cases and some 27,000 deaths, and Spain had reported more than 232,000 cases and more than 23,800 fatalities.

> "What makes me most angry is that we had a month and a half to get ready after our first case, and we had weeks to prepare after watching what's happened in Italy."[8]
>
> —Ángela Hernández Puente, a Spanish labor leader

As the pandemic spread throughout Europe, leaders of Spain and Italy received criticism from public health officials for not realizing the dangers posed by COVID-19. Critics charged that leaders of the two countries let public activities in Spain and Italy go on too long before they issued stay-at-home orders and similar measures to stem the spread of the disease. Italy did not issue its stay-at-home order until March 10, and Spain waited until March 15 to order citizens to remain in their homes. "What makes me most angry is that we had a month and a half to get ready after our first case, and we had weeks to prepare after watching what's happened in Italy,"[8] said Ángela Hernández Puente, a leader of a health care worker labor union in the Spanish capital of Madrid.

Lockdowns Across Europe

For citizens of Italy and Spain, as well as other European countries, the lockdowns were difficult to endure. Spain and Italy are both known for their lively nightlife, where people dine late in the evening and congregate in crowded bars. But even for those raising young children in Europe, the stay-at-home orders meant dramatic changes to their lifestyles.

Cristina Higgins, an American university professor living in Bergamo, Italy, said many of her friends fell ill from the disease before the stay-at-home orders were issued. "We have friends who are getting sick. It's very stressful," Higgins said. "I am nauseous all day long, because every time I look at the news or talk to somebody else, something terrible has happened. And I don't know what's going to happen next."[9]

During the pandemic, Higgins, her husband, and their three young children rarely ventured outside past the driveway of their apartment building. Their children's school provided lessons through videoconferencing over the internet. Homework was assigned and turned in through e-mail. At night, the family played Monopoly and other board games. The only trip Higgins's husband made away from home was a once-a-week visit to a local grocery store. Patrons were ordered to remain several feet apart from one another—a concept known as social distancing—to minimize

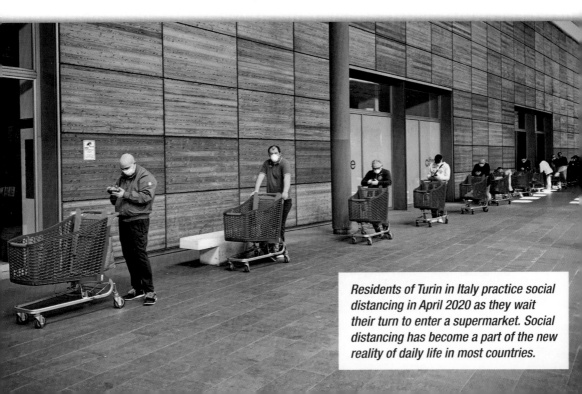

Residents of Turin in Italy practice social distancing in April 2020 as they wait their turn to enter a supermarket. Social distancing has become a part of the new reality of daily life in most countries.

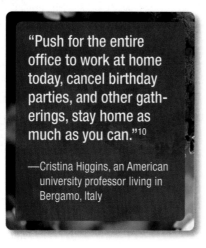
the likelihood that they could infect others if they had already contracted the disease but were not yet showing symptoms.

As Higgins and her family endured the lockdown in Italy, she posted a message on her Facebook page, warning people in America and elsewhere that they would soon be experiencing the same type of life under a nationwide lockdown. Moreover, she pointed out that hospitals and other care providers needed time to prepare for the huge influx of COVID-19 patients that was sure to come:

> You have a chance to make a difference and stop the spread in your country. Push for the entire office to work at home today, cancel birthday parties, and other gatherings, stay home as much as you can. If you have a fever, any fever, stay home. Push for school closures, now. Anything you can do to stop the spread, because it is spreading in your communities—there is a two-week incubation period—and if you do these things now you can buy your medical system time.[10]

COVID-19 Spreads to America

Back in the United States, the steps taken by national leaders to stop the spread of the disease soon proved to be inadequate. For example, on January 31, President Donald Trump issued an order prohibiting travelers who had visited China during the previous two weeks from entering the United States. But that effort fell short of curbing the spread of the virus. In the United States, the disease took its first victim when a patient in Santa Clara County, California, died on February 6.

Nonetheless, for the first few weeks of March, most Americans went about their lives, wondering whether the severe mea-

Typical symptoms of COVID-19 include a cough, shortness of breath, fever, chills, muscle pain, sore throat, and a headache. People with influenza often experience these same symptoms. However, COVID-19 has one other common symptom not found in the typical flu case: temporary loss of taste and smell.

The condition is known as anosmia. With other illnesses caused by coronaviruses, patients have reported losing both senses of taste and smell for several months. One study found that to be particularly true for people who contracted SARS (severe acute respiratory syndrome) also caused by a coronavirus. The study cited the case of a Taiwanese woman afflicted with anosmia for two years after her recovery from SARS. With COVID-19, however, regaining those senses appears to occur within weeks. "The good news is that the symptoms seem to be self-limiting and improve with time," says Wendy Smith, a physician who specializes in diseases of the ears and throat. "Cases related to COVID-19 may resolve more quickly."

Still, some victims report they found losing their senses of smell and taste truly frightening. "I woke up and couldn't taste or smell anything," says Holly Bourne, a COVID-19 patient from London, England. "[It was] one of the most upsetting things I've ever gone through because you're not in the driving seat . . . I just feel really powerless and scared."

Quoted in Angela N. Baldwin, "COVID-19 Symptoms May Include Altered Senses of Smell, Taste," ABC News, March 24, 2020. https://abcnews.go.com.

Quoted in Sarah Dean, "Many People Lost Their Sense of Smell Weeks Ago. They're Still Waiting for It to Come Back," CNN, April 12, 2020. www.cnn.com.

sures imposed in Asia, Europe, and elsewhere would find their way into their communities. They got their answer on March 19, when California governor Gavin Newsom announced a statewide lockdown, ordering nonessential businesses to close and everyone to stay home. New York governor Andrew Cuomo acted a day later, announcing a state lockdown commencing March 22.

Other governors soon joined Newsom and Cuomo. By mid-April, forty-two states had issued stay-at-home orders. The other states had either issued partial stay-at-home orders or had left it up to individual communities to issue their own orders, and many did. By mid-April it was estimated that 95 percent of the US population was living under stay-at-home orders.

Despite the lockdown orders, the disease took its toll. By early May, state governments had reported that more than 1.2 million Americans were infected with the disease, and there were more than sixty-nine thousand fatalities. Just some three months after the virus became zoonotic, jumping from a bat or a pangolin to a shopper at the Wuhan wet market, COVID-19 had spread its deadly tentacles across the globe.

Life Under the Lockdown

In late March 2020, as the pandemic swept across the country, the scene unfolding outside the Safeway supermarket in Flagstaff, Arizona, was turning out to be quite typical. At 6 a.m., three hours before the store's normal opening time, senior citizens started lining up to enter the store. Many had a single product on their shopping lists: toilet paper.

The Safeway in Flagstaff was one of many stores across the country that reserved early morning hours for senior citizens to shop. Believed to be particularly vulnerable to COVID-19, people over the age of sixty-five were permitted by supermarkets to shop before normal opening times so they could avoid large crowds and, therefore, minimize their chances of becoming infected with the disease. But it also gave the older shoppers opportunities to obtain products that were in short supply due to the pandemic; in most places, it seemed the one product in shortest supply was toilet paper. As she entered the Safeway, shopper Lisa Roberts told a reporter, "Even now, this is the second, third or fourth time I've come here and can't find what I need. I need more hand sanitizer and toilet paper, but they never have it. I'm hoping today I'll get lucky."[11] As it turned out, the Safeway had received a shipment of

toilet paper shortly before Roberts arrived, and she found the shelves full of the product. She bought two packages.

For months, toilet paper and other products became increasingly hard to find on store shelves. One reason for the shortages was due to the fear that dominated the minds of many shoppers: believing that the pandemic would keep them locked up for months, many shoppers resorted to panic buying. They bought much more of certain products, such as toilet paper, than they ordinarily needed. This attitude helped lead to shortages on store shelves.

According to Andrew Stephen, a professor of marketing at the University of Oxford in Great Britain, people often resort to panic buying in times of crises as a way of psychologically giving themselves control over their situation. By stocking up on toilet

Nearly empty store shelves greet shoppers at a Georgia supermarket in March 2020. Toilet paper, disinfecting wipes, flour, rice, and ramen were among the products most likely to be the focus of panic buying.

paper, he explained, they believe they will be better able to endure the crisis if they know they will never run out of a product that is vital to living a normal life. "People are really not equipped psychologically to process this type of thing," said Stephen. "So that just makes it worse for a lot of people in terms of uncertainty, and then they do whatever they need to do to try and get back some control."[12]

Overwhelmed Delivery Services

For months, the majority of America's 331 million people were on lockdown—most of them rarely venturing outside their homes except for the vital tasks of buying groceries and other supplies. And when they did leave their homes, they found themselves ordered by their state governments to follow social distancing guidelines established by the US Centers for Disease Control and Prevention (CDC). The guidelines required people to wear cloth masks outside their homes so their breaths would be shielded from others. The guidelines called for people to remain at least 6 feet (1.8 m) apart. Wearing disposable rubber gloves was also recommended to help keep germs off hands and fingers, with the gloves tossed in the trash after one use.

To enter a grocery store, people typically lined up outside, standing on markers painted along the sidewalk to maintain social distancing. Security guards waved handfuls of shoppers at a time into the stores. Exiting a Walmart in Bloomingdale, Illinois, on March 28, shopper Melinda Derer told a reporter that her experience in the store was nothing like a normal trip to a Walmart—that is, crowded, with bustling shoppers in every aisle. "It's quieter," she commented. "People are . . . taking what they need and getting out."[13]

But many people feared even going out for brief trips to grocery stores. Grocery delivery services such as Instacart, Dash, and Boxed soon became overwhelmed. Ordinarily, the services provide shoppers for people unable to get out to the stores themselves. Customers make use of apps developed by the shopping services, which assign workers to move through the stores, filling carts with the orders, then dropping the groceries outside customers' homes. Prior to the pandemic, the services typically offered either same-day or next-day delivery, but after the start of the pandemic, the delivery services were inundated with orders. People attempting to use delivery services were typically told they could not expect their orders to be filled for two weeks or more.

Moreover, the delivery services were further slowed because of panic buying—many customers wanted to buy several weeks' worth of groceries out of fear they would not be able to use the service again for an extended period. Such big orders further slowed down the services because the workers were spending much longer than usual in filling each order. According to Alexa Dash, director of marketing for Dash, "Originally we used to be able to order four days out, now we have it up to 10 days out and we are booked solid pretty much 10 days out. I've noticed the order sizes have like skyrocketed so instead of the average order being $100, $150, we're seeing orders of $500 and up for one order."[14]

Neighbors Helping Neighbors

Given the long lines awaiting them to get into the stores, or waits of up to two weeks for Instacart or Dash deliveries, many people found they simply could not find groceries on their own. In many cases, friends and neighbors stepped in to help out, often coming to the aid of elderly neighbors who did not want to risk trips to the supermarket even in the early morning hours set aside for them to shop in the less-crowded stores.

In San Francisco, Mia Ludovico used social media to let her neighbors know that she was available to do their grocery shopping for them if they did not feel safe going into stores. "I realized that not everybody is so lucky to feel like they'll be able to go to the grocery store and go grocery shopping," Ludovico said. "I figured I'd reach out to neighbors to see if they need any help."[15]

Others offered to walk dogs, mow lawns, and do other outdoor chores for shut-ins—all performed while following social distancing guidelines. On April 18, New Jersey governor Phil Mur-

Prison inmates, who are typically forced to share tight quarters, were considered particularly susceptible to COVID-19. After all, it was virtually impossible for most prison inmates to maintain the CDC's recommended social distancing guidelines while living in small prison cells. "We are living three feet apart, in bunk beds, like a dormitory," said Anh Do, a seventy-nine-year-old inmate in a Texas prison who had been convicted on fraud charges. "I'm at very high risk. If one person gets sick, it's like a death sentence in here."

Therefore, as the pandemic spread throughout America, many governors authorized the early release of inmates. The inmates who were released early were either found to be nearing the ends of their sentences or were serving sentences for nonviolent offenses.

Prior to the pandemic, about 2.3 million Americans were being held in county, state, and federal prisons. By the spring of 2020, no estimate had been placed on the number of inmates who were granted early release due to the pandemic, but some jails offered glimpses of the national trend. In Cuyahoga County, Ohio, for example, the county jail population dropped from about 1,900 to less than 1,300. In Mercer County, Pennsylvania, 60 of the county jail's 308 inmates were released. Peter C. Acker, the district attorney of Mercer County, said his office would not pursue jail terms for many new offenders: "We're not putting low-level punks in jail at the moment."

Quoted in Kimberly Kindy, Emma Brown, and Dalton Bennett, "'Disaster Waiting to Happen': Thousands of Inmates Released as Jails and Prisons Face Coronavirus Threat," *Washington Post*, March 25, 2020. www.washingtonpost.com.

phy used his daily press update to praise twelve-year-old Dominic Mercado of Vineland, New Jersey, for celebrating his birthday by collecting food to donate to a local food bank that distributes groceries to the needy. Murphy said, "Dominic, we wish you the very happiest of birthdays and we thank you."[16]

Streaming Services Explode

Whether people were afraid of venturing out of their homes at all, or they limited their trips outside to weekly visits to their grocery stores, it was clear that the pandemic had dramatically changed life in America. The once-bustling streets of big cities were virtually abandoned during the pandemic. Sporting events that typically occurred in arenas and stadiums packed with tens of thousands of fans were canceled, among them the National College Athletic Association's annual college men's and women's basketball championship tournaments. The Little League World Series in Williamsport, Pennsylvania, was canceled. The National Hockey League and the National Basketball Association—each entering the final few weeks of their seasons and approaching their league playoffs when the lockdowns were announced—were forced to suspend play. Major League Baseball postponed the start of its season, just days before pitchers were ready to face their first batters. On March 24, the International Olympic Committee announced it would postpone the 2020 Summer Olympic Games, originally slated to begin July 24 in Tokyo, Japan, until 2021. Meanwhile, pop concerts were canceled. Broadway theaters closed. Movie theaters closed. Premiere dates for new films were postponed.

People were forced to find activities to do at home, and that often meant sitting in front of their television sets for hours as they focused on the offerings of streaming services such as Netflix. During the first three months of 2020, Netflix announced that it had added 16 million new viewers to its service. Moreover, a new television streaming service, Disney+—created by the entertainment giant Walt Disney Company—announced that it had quickly surged to 50 million subscribers during the first few months of 2020. The service had only been established in November 2019, just weeks before the COVID-19 pandemic arrived in the United States.

Still, the lockdowns were hard to endure, particularly on young people who found they could no longer be with their friends. Christopher Shelton, a fifteen-year-old freshman at Haverford Senior High School in suburban Philadelphia, said he missed playing his trombone in the high school band, and he also missed spending time with his girlfriend. "Band is like family," he commented, "and you lose a little of that when it goes away." He did manage to connect with his girlfriend through the FaceTime app on his phone, but he said that experience fell short of actually being together with her. "It's annoying when you can't hang out,"[17] he said.

Lockdowns Slowly Ease

By late April, many people found they could endure the national lockdown no longer. Protests broke out in several American cities. Known as "You Can't Close America" rallies, the gatherings were organized on social media. On April 18, dozens of protesters attended a rally in downtown Austin, Texas. Many of the protesters wore cloth masks across their faces, but a large number chose not to do so. They hugged one another, shook hands, and demanded that their state government end the lockdown.

In April 2020 residents of Redlands, California, protest the lockdown and demand that businesses be allowed to reopen. In cities where protests took place, participants often refused to wear masks or practice social distancing.

"I don't fear a potential pathogen [virus]," said protester David Litrell. "I think there's potential pathogens around us all the time, and for the most part, we're healthy."[18]

Some governors sympathized with the protesters and took steps to reopen their states in late April, including provisions for people to pursue leisure activities outside their homes. They cited statistics indicating that the COVID-19 infection rates in their states had declined as rationale for these decisions.

"I think there's potential pathogens around us all the time, and for the most part, we're healthy."[18]

—David Litrell, a protester in Austin, Texas

In the last week of April, Florida reopened its beaches, albeit with restrictions: people were required to maintain social distancing while using the beaches, and no congregating of beachgoers was permitted. Georgia permitted a number of leisure activities to restart in late April, among them the reopening of bowling alleys. These steps were taken despite warnings from public health officials that allowing people to engage in leisure activities outside their homes could lead to new spikes in infections.

After spending the better part of two months locked in their homes, watching the available rolls of toilet paper dwindle in their bathroom cabinets, many Americans were desperate for a change. When the governors began opening up their states, some stayed put—believing that the danger had not passed. Others rejoiced and tried to return to at least some of the life they knew before the pandemic.

CHAPTER THREE

Struggling Workers and Businesses

By January 2020, Marek and Kothney-Issa Bush, both twenty-eight, emerged from years of staggering debt. Together, the Bushes had been living under as much as $125,000 of debt owed for student loans, car loans, and credit card balances. Married since 2014, the couple from Dallas, Texas, worked hard to pay off their debt. Marek was a fraud investigator for a national retailer, and Kothney-Issa worked as a restaurant server. They gave up frivolous spending, did not travel, rarely enjoyed dinner out at restaurants, lived in a modest home, and took second jobs; Marek delivered pizzas, and Kothney-Issa worked evenings as a tutor. By working hard and saving, they managed to put money away each month to pay down their debt. Now debt free, the Bushes looked forward to starting new lives in 2020 released from the burden of owing money.

But then the COVID-19 pandemic swept through the country. The retailer that employed Marek was forced to close its stores, and he was laid off. Both restaurants where Kothney-Issa worked also closed. Under the Texas lockdown order, restaurants could offer only takeout food; therefore, the restaurants had no need to employ her as a server. By the spring of 2020, the Bushes were living off the five thousand dollars they had managed to save since paying off their debt just months earlier. Interviewed by a reporter in April, Marek said he and his wife hoped to make their savings last until the end of the pandemic, when they could return to work; otherwise, he worried, they may be forced to go back into debt. He commented, "We've got to keep fighting financially and keep striving to get to a more stable place, because a lot of the things that we feel security in can be gone in an instant."[19]

The Bushes were not alone in losing their jobs and financial security due to the pandemic. Prior to the outbreak, the national unemployment rate in America was 3.5 percent—a historic low. It meant that 96.5 percent of Americans were employed and drawing salaries. By the end of May 2020, the unemployment rate skyrocketed to more than 23.9 percent with more than 40 million Americans out of work. The high unemployment plunged the nation into what is known as a recession—a period in which unemployment is

CLOSED DUE TO COVID 19 CORONAVIRUS

As happened with thousands of other businesses deemed nonessential, this gym closed during the shutdown. Business closings led to an unprecedented number of layoffs—throwing more than 40 million Americans out of work.

The COVID-19 pandemic hit small business owners hard. If their businesses were deemed nonessential, owners were forced to close their doors. Even essential businesses that found ways to remain open were forced to overcome numerous obstacles.

During the pandemic, restaurants were permitted to remain open but to offer takeout service only, usually by making meals available through curbside pickups—meaning customers could pick up their meals outside the restaurants. In Seattle, Washington, Clay and Robin Martin opened a small restaurant in 2014 that they named Hello Robin. It specialized in baked goods created by Robin. When the pandemic hit, the Martins closed the restaurant to diners but kept a takeout window open. While business did decline, the Martins were able to keep their workers employed, all of whom were part-time employees. And their landlord told them not to worry about making rental payments until the pandemic passed. Still, plans by the Martins to open a second restaurant in a new location were put on hold.

Elsewhere in Seattle, more than forty-five hundred other small businesses closed during the pandemic. Robin Martin said she and her husband never considered closing Hello Robin. She said the couple felt a responsibility to their customers to remain open. "I feel like it's a civic duty to be open right now," she said. "We're clinging for any little bit of hope, trying to be as optimistic as we can."

Quoted in Andrea Riquier, "These Small-Business Owners Made Their Dreams Come True—and Then the Coronavirus Hit," MarketWatch, April 27, 2020. www.marketwatch.com.

high, production is low, and people are hesitant to spend money. As Diane Swonk, a Chicago-based economist, asserted, "There's nowhere to hide. This is the deepest, fastest, most broad-based recession we've ever seen."[20]

Challenges Facing Workers

The Bushes lost their jobs because neither was categorized as an essential worker. To keep working, they would have needed to be employed in jobs deemed vital to maintaining the health and safety of Americans during the pandemic. Essential workers included health care workers, such as physicians, nurses, and emergency medical technicians. But workers deemed vital to American society also included supermarket clerks, auto mechanics, bus drivers and other transit workers, airport employees, delivery drivers, janitors, trash collectors, and postal employees.

Although these workers were able to keep their jobs and earn salaries, they still faced daunting challenges. Many were asked to work several hours of overtime each week to meet the high demands of the citizens forced to stay home under the lockdown orders. Plus, while doing their jobs, these workers were com-

Protected by a plastic shield, gloves, and a mask, a cashier scans items being purchased. Grocery and big box store workers were among those who put in long hours and risked exposure to the virus while doing jobs considered essential.

ing in contact with people who might be carrying the virus. Matt Monaghan, a New York bus driver, said, "I myself have anxiety, when people are on the bus, of catching this thing. We have families to go home to and we don't want to bring it home to our families."[21] Monaghan's fears were confirmed when, in early April, officials in New York City disclosed that eight city transit workers had died from COVID-19.

In some cases, whole cities were impacted when essential workers were infected. In Sioux Falls, South Dakota, more than eight hundred of the thirty-seven hundred workers at the Smithfield Foods plant fell ill from COVID-19. The plant prepares and packages pork for shipments to grocery stores and, therefore, the Smithfield workers were regarded as essential employees. Moreover, in addition to the eight hundred workers who fell ill at the plant, state officials disclosed that 90 percent of South Dakota's twenty-three hundred positive cases were in Minnehaha and Lincoln Counties, which surround Sioux Falls. About half of those cases were believed to have been directly linked to the workers who spent their shifts in the Smithfield plant, then went home and inadvertently infected others. After the outbreak at the Smithfield plant was reported, the facility was closed and all of its employees were laid off.

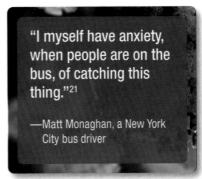

"I myself have anxiety, when people are on the bus, of catching this thing."[21]

—Matt Monaghan, a New York City bus driver

The Smithfield plant was long regarded as a place where immigrants who fled war or poverty in their home countries could find employment in the United States. One of those workers was Achut Deng, a refugee from Sudan. Before the pandemic struck the plant, Deng routinely put in eleven-hour days, six days a week, to provide for her family of three children. While working at the plant, Deng fell victim to COVID-19. She recovered and was anxious to get back to work when Smithfield Foods decided to close the plant. With the plant closed, Deng worried whether her coworkers would find ways to survive. She said, "This company does a lot of things when it comes to families, supporting families. Most of them, they don't know how to speak English, they don't know how to read, where can they go after that? Where can they go and provide for the needs of their families?"[22]

The Economic Stimulus Program

When the Smithfield workers were laid off, they joined millions of Americans who lost their jobs. Early in the pandemic, the US government stepped in to provide assistance. When a worker is laid off, he or she is usually entitled to unemployment compensation. This is financial help provided by the government to assist with paying bills until the person finds a new job. Typically, unemployment compensation payments are capped at twenty-six weeks, but in March 2020 the US Congress added thirteen weeks to the benefit. Moreover, Congress approved a $2 trillion economic stimulus program to provide aid to businesses to help them stay afloat during the pandemic as well as one-time payments to taxpayers, whether they were unemployed or still held their jobs. The aid included payments of $1200 per person as well as an extra $500 per child if the taxpayers had children aged sixteen or younger.

Still, for many laid-off workers, the extra cash from unemployment benefits as well as the one-time stimulus payments were not enough to meet their needs. Some could no longer afford groceries and were forced to line up at food banks to receive boxes of food donated by city governments, community organizations, and private donors. In the resort community of Atlantic City, New Jersey, the city's seven casino hotels employed more than twenty-seven thousand workers. All of them lost their jobs when the businesses were forced to close during the pandemic. One of those workers was bartender Diego Ramirez, who took his place in line at a city food bank. "It's a little help," Ramirez said as he waited in line. "I just hope [the casinos] open quick, but safely."[23]

Kimberly Horton, a mother of two from Jackson, Mississippi, received $1700 in the stimulus program. She qualified for the extra $500 for her thirteen-year-old son but not for her daughter, Tyra, a college student. Although Tyra's classes were transitioned to online sessions, she elected to stay in her apartment near the campus at Mississippi State University in Starkville, about 90 miles (145 km) from Jackson. Tyra had been working part-time at a retail store near campus, but she lost her job when the store closed due to the pandemic. Horton used her stimulus check to help her daughter pay her bills. "It is hard to keep her afloat right now and keep my son and I in good shape," Horton said. "But I was able to send her money as soon as I saw it come in."[24]

Working in Her Pajamas

Horton was actually a lot more fortunate than many other workers. Although her employer closed its office, Horton, a payroll administrator, was able to work from home during the pandemic. Across the country, as thousands of businesses closed their offices, many were able to keep going because their workers could use their laptops and phones to keep operations moving. No longer was it necessary for them to commute to work in the morning and spend their days within the confines of their cubicles. Now, they found they could do their jobs at their kitchen tables. By late spring of 2020, economists had not yet estimated the number of people carrying out their duties at home, but experts believed it was much higher than the 3 percent of the workforce—about 5 million workers—who worked at home prior to the pandemic.

> "The hardest part of working from home for me is missing out on the networking and camaraderie with colleagues."[25]
>
> —Shannon Curtis, who worked at home during the pandemic

Shannon Curtis, a clinical dietician in Galveston, Texas, was also able to work from home. Employed by a local hospital, her job involved planning patient diets, which she could do on her laptop. Often working in her pajamas, Curtis was able to remotely provide the data needed by the kitchen workers to prepare meals for the patients. "Right now, I just feel blessed to still have a job," said Curtis. "The hardest part of working from home for me is missing out on the networking and camaraderie with colleagues. I enjoyed being in my office most of the time, but I also enjoyed chatting with co-workers at lunch or in their offices as well. It's just different now."[25]

Clearly, the COVID-19 pandemic brought a new normal to the nation's economy. Many people lost their jobs and were forced to depend on food banks. Others were able to keep their jobs by working at home. But many others were deemed to be essential employees, meaning they reported for work and often faced extremely long days as well as a heightened possibility that they could be infected with COVID-19.

CHAPTER FOUR

Schools Close Their Doors

For many school students in America, the highlight of their senior year is prom—the chance to get dressed up, dine and dance with their friends, and look ahead to what awaits them after high school. "I was super excited for senior prom," said Kaya Koraleski, an eighteen-year-old senior at Central High School in Omaha, Nebraska.

> Prom is pretty much a rite of culture for Omaha kids. It's the big night to get super dressed up. It's always been a huge thing to go out and buy your dress early. I got my dress in December or January. . . . I found the perfect one. I have this navy blue, long, super sparkly dress, because I wanted a dress with the themes of the Roaring 20s, which is the theme of our year. I had my hair figured out in February. It's a very indescribable feeling, getting ready for a big event that you know you're going to remember for the rest of your life.[26]

But school districts in Nebraska started closing schools in the second week of March to protect students and faculty members against the spread of COVID-19. And on April 1, Nebraska governor Pete Ricketts announced all schools would remain closed at least through May 31. Several other governors went further,

Happy high school seniors pose for a photo with friends on prom night. Thousands of high school seniors were denied this opportunity when their proms, and even most graduation ceremonies, were canceled because of COVID-19.

closing schools until the end of the school year in June. Most school districts continued to provide online classes to students, but all other school activities—among them sports and clubs—were canceled. For Koraleski and other students, it meant their senior proms were canceled as well. "I feel like the world has kind of skipped over us, and forgotten how big of a deal your senior year can be," commented Olivia Mathews, a seventeen-year-old senior at Marian High School in Omaha. "When everything started to get canceled, I was like, can't we postpone it? Because this is it for me. I'm not going to be able to do this ever again."[27]

By late April, public and private schools in all fifty states as well as Washington, DC, had either been ordered closed by

> "I feel like the world has kind of skipped over us, and forgotten how big of a deal your senior year can be."[27]
>
> —Olivia Mathews, a senior at Marian High School in Omaha, Nebraska

their governors or closed voluntarily by administrators after public health officials recommended classes be canceled. The closures affected nearly 55 million school students in the nation's 118,000 public and private schools.

Learning at Home

Although the school buildings were closed, most schools continued to provide online classes using applications such as Zoom, Skype, Google Meet, Google Hangout, and Google Classroom. These apps enabled teachers to lead classes from home, have face time with students, monitor their at-home learning, and assign homework. Still, many teachers found the experience of leading classes from their kitchen tables challenging. Thu Nguyen, a sixth-grade teacher at Sidwell Friends School in Washington, DC, said she soon found herself overwhelmed by her students' questions, which they submitted through e-mails. "I can't respond to 33 kids in writing fast enough," Nguyen explained. "I was getting emails—question after question from one particular student—you know, like 10 emails in five minutes. And I was like, 'This is not going to work.'"[28]

Many teachers reserved parts of the day to have face time with their students, either in one-on-one or group sessions. Hannah Klumpe, a seventh-grade social studies teacher at Berea Middle School in Greenville, South Carolina, set up daily Google Hangout sessions with students. "They can pop in if I have any questions or if they need help with something," she said. "I can read some directions aloud to them. . . . [I'm] just making sure that my kids are OK during this very crazy time." Klumpe added, "Teaching through a computer is not why I became a teacher. I became a teacher to build relationships with my students and that one-on-one, face-to-face interaction, I think, is what I really miss."[29]

"I became a teacher to build relationships with my students and that one-on-one, face-to-face interaction, I think, is what I really miss."[29]

—Hannah Klumpe, a seventh-grade social studies teacher at Berea Middle School in Greenville, South Carolina

A student uses her laptop to interact with her teacher. When schools closed because of the pandemic, teachers and students nationwide shifted to online, or distance, learning.

Students also acknowledged the challenges of trying to learn at home. Danny Peng, a thirteen-year-old student at William Alexander Middle School in New York City, said, "Me and my friends often have to work for quite a long time, like at least five hours on all the assignments. It's really boring to read the lesson info by yourself and then apply it to your assignments. I feel like this is the hard part."[30] Another student, sixteen-year old Alexis Jennings of Woods High School in Houston, Texas, found that there are simply some subjects that cannot be taught online. She commented, "Since my school has started online class it's been harder to motivate myself to work and pay attention. I also miss my art elective. We had our first online art class today and it was only 20 minutes long which was strange because it's usually two hours."[31]

"Since my school has started online class it's been harder to motivate myself to work and pay attention."[31]

—Alexis Jennings, a student at Woods High School in Houston, Texas

Shrinking Class Sizes

As schools transitioned to online classes, many teachers found their class sizes shrinking. In Los Angeles, for example, school officials reported that a third of the city's school students—about forty-thousand students—were not making daily contact with their teachers. Moreover, an additional fifteen thousand students had never logged on to their online classes since the district closed its schools on March 16. "It's simply not acceptable that we lose touch with 15,000 young adults or that many students aren't getting the education they should be," asserted Austin Beutner, the superintendent of schools in Los Angeles. "This will take some time and a good bit of trial and error to get it right. And it will

College Students Struggle at Home

As the COVID-19 pandemic spread through America, more than eleven hundred American college campuses closed, affecting about 14 million students. Many of the schools elected to continue their classes online, but many college students found challenges in learning at home while staring at computer screens. "I would not say I'm enjoying it," said Madison Selby, a twenty-one-year-old senior at the University of Washington in Seattle. Shortly after her school closed its campus on March 9, Selby returned home to Orange County, California, where she finished her classes online.

Spencer Hagaman, a twenty-one-year-old Yale University junior, returned home to Huntington Beach, California, after Yale closed its campus in New Haven, Connecticut, on March 10. Hagaman continued to take his classes online but found many distractions at home. He pointed out that a lot of his classes involve more than just following lectures. His professors encourage students to exchange ideas—and that proved to be a challenge for classes conducted over the internet. "You're going to have parents screaming in the background, 'Breakfast is ready,' that sort of thing," Hagaman said. "I would hypothesize that most students are going to want to be in the classroom."

Quoted in Matt Krupnick, "Forced Off Campus by Coronavirus, Students Aren't Won Over by Online Education," *NewsHour*, PBS, March 27, 2020. www.pbs.org.

take the continued patience and commitment of all involved—students, families and teachers."[32]

It soon became obvious to school officials why so many students were not logging in to their online classes. Many low-income students lacked access to the technology they needed to continue their classes at home. Their families could not afford to buy laptops, which cost several hundred dollars. Many school districts were able to step in and provide laptops to low-income students, but the students faced other challenges. Titilayo Alu-ko, eighteen, a junior at Landmark High School in New York City, was issued a laptop by her high school, but her family could not afford an internet connection at home. "I actually need my

Students make use of a library Wi-Fi connection to work on a school assignment. Thousands of students with no internet at home lost out when both schools and public libraries were forced to close.

teachers, who know me and understand me, to help me, and I don't have that," she said. "I just keep thinking, 'Oh, my God, I might not pass.' I'm just really scared for the future."[33] And since the lockdown orders applied to places that ordinarily provide free Wi-Fi—libraries, coffee shops, bookstores, and office supply stores—these students had no place left to go to make connections with their online classes.

The lack of access to technology was not limited to students in urban school districts like Los Angeles and New York. Students in rural parts of America also had difficulty connecting to their schools and teachers online. Many rural households lack internet connections. In rural Alaska, for example, teacher Corey Shepherd estimated that half of his students do not have access to reliable internet service. "Internet service is very expensive in rural Alaska and comes with data caps," Shepherd said. "Internet service is also prone to interruptions due to weather."[34] Shepherd and other teachers in Alaska took some extra steps to help their students connect: they delivered work to their students' homes and set up mobile Wi-Fi hot spots in places like parking lots, where students could gather with their laptops and participate in classes while still maintaining social distancing rules. Shepherd also spent a lot of time during the day on the phone with his students, answering their questions about their classwork.

Challenges Faced by Special Education Students

Perhaps the young people most affected by the school shutdowns were the nation's more than 6 million special education students. These are students who, because of developmental or physical disabilities, need to receive one-on-one help in learning from teachers and teachers' aides. For example, Marla Murasko's son Jacob was born with Down syndrome, which has hindered Jacob's physical and intellectual development. Lessons must be tailored specifically to his needs, and he often needs one-on-one help from a teacher or aide to understand his lessons. His teachers in Hopkinton, Massachusetts, sent his work home, but Murasko found herself challenged as to how to present the information to Jacob and help him learn the material. "It has been very frustrating for us," she said. "He can't look at a five-page worksheet and learn. He needs it very simplified in order for him to learn it. If there's no accommodations or modifications for him, he really can't attend to that lesson plan unless I modify it for him."[35]

For the first few weeks that her school district closed in suburban St. Louis, Missouri, special education teacher Ann Hiebert

Philanthropists Step In

Given the challenges of providing online learning to students from low-income families, many school districts ultimately elected to cease classes altogether—to provide no online instruction at all. School officials and political leaders determined it would be unfair to provide education to students whose families could afford the technology needed to maintain classes while denying other students those opportunities.

For example, city officials in Philadelphia closed schools on March 13, then announced four days later that the schools would not provide online classes because many students lacked access to laptop computers or internet connections. A few days later, Brian and Aileen Roberts donated $5 million to the school district to buy laptops for low-income students. Brian is the chief executive officer (CEO) of Comcast—the cable television and internet provider headquartered in the city. "When we heard that many Philadelphia students weren't going to be able to learn from home without laptops, we quickly decided we wanted to help and provide these teachers, parents and students with the technology they need to begin learning online within just a few weeks," the couple said in a statement. "In good times or bad, now all of our Philadelphia students will have access to technology to help them succeed." Students started receiving their laptops in early April. Online classes commenced for all students in the city on April 20.

Quoted in NBC 10, "Comcast CEO, Family Give $5M to Buy Laptops for Philly Students," March 27, 2020. www.nbcphiladelphia.com.

tried to teach her classes online to her disabled students. She soon concluded that the students were not progressing, so she shifted her strategy. She designed her lessons for the students' parents, showing them how to present the information to the students. She produced her own videos at home, explaining the lessons, then made the videos available to the parents over the internet. "I'm trying to be more of a resource to parents,"[36] she explained.

When the 2019–2020 school year began, it looked to be like any other. Students went to their classes. Interscholastic sports were played. The chess clubs and debate societies met, and the cheerleading squads held practices. And before long, students like Kaya Koraleski started looking for the outfits they planned to wear to their senior proms. By the time the school year had ended, however, it was clear that this school year would be unlike any other. For many students, their school days ended locked at home, away from the friends with whom they had shared so many important moments over the years.

Hospitals and Health Care Workers Fight the Pandemic

Madhvi Ayi immigrated to America in 1994, making her home in the New York City suburb of Floral Park. She had been a physician in her native India. After arriving in America, she found a job as a physician assistant at the Woodhull Medical Center, a hospital in New York City. As a physician assistant, she was able to perform minor procedures on patients, such as physical examinations, diagnosing minor illnesses, and assisting doctors in surgeries. A typical job for a physician assistant would be to diagnose and treat a flu sufferer whose symptoms were severe enough to merit emergency room care. And so, as COVID-19 swept through New York City in the early months of 2020, Ayi found her days dominated with patients suffering from the disease. Very early in the pandemic she started putting in twelve-hour shifts at the hospital.

Woodhull had been inundated with patients—so many, in fact, that the hospital had been forced to convert several wards into makeshift intensive care units. But in the first few weeks of 2020, when doctors were unsure of how the disease spread from person to person, health care workers were not instructed to take precautions—to wear masks that would shield them from the germs floating throughout the hospital air. Not until March 17 were Woodhull employees instructed to wear masks. Five days earlier, as Ayi was completing a shift in one of the hospital's COVID-19 units, she began coughing.

Ayi was diagnosed with COVID-19. She stayed home, but her symptoms grew worse. Three days after her diagnosis, Ayi's husband, Raj, drove her to the Long Island Jewish Medical Center near the couple's home. She was admitted, but over the next week her condition continued to deteriorate. As she became desperately ill, locked away from her family at the hospital, Ayi exchanged texts with her daughter Minnoli, a student at the University of Buffalo in upstate New York who had returned home to resume her classes online. In one text, Minnoli wrote to her mother:

> [Minnoli:] "Hi mommy. College is getting so much more stressful now that it's at home. . . . The good thing is I'm home but I need you to come back here to me. I hope you ate dinner and I'm still praying for you and haven't gave up hope."
>
> [Ayi:] "Concentrate.". . .
>
> [Minnoli:] "I am but I want u home."
>
> [Ayi:] "Home soon."
>
> [Minnoli:] "I love you mommy with all my heart."
>
> [Ayi:] "Love you."[37]

That was the last text Minnoli received from her mother. Ayi died a short time later, on March 29, 2020.

Health Care Workers at Risk

The sad case of Madhvi Ayi illustrates the stresses facing the American health care system as COVID-19 swept through the country.

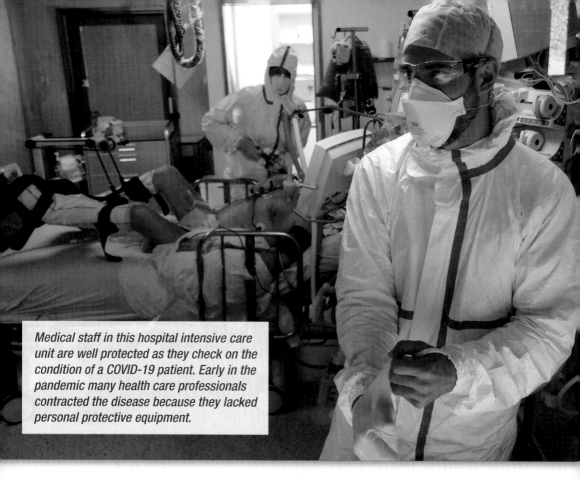

Medical staff in this hospital intensive care unit are well protected as they check on the condition of a COVID-19 patient. Early in the pandemic many health care professionals contracted the disease because they lacked personal protective equipment.

Hospitals were largely unprepared for the inundation of patients. They lacked the test kits to determine whether patients had truly been infected with the disease or were merely suffering from the flu. They lacked the beds to house the most serious cases. Many hospitals lacked a sufficient number of ventilators to help the sickest patients breathe. And as the Ayi case shows, many health care workers were themselves stricken with COVID-19. On April 14, the CDC reported that nearly ten thousand health care workers had been infected with the virus. Of those, the CDC reported that twenty-seven had died from the illness. Some groups have disputed that number. National Nurses United, which represents nearly 200,000 nurses in the United States, reported that at least 48 nurses had died from COVID-19. Moreover, the International Council of Nurses, a group based in Ankara, Turkey, that represents nurses worldwide, released global statistics in May reporting more than ninety thousand health care workers had contracted the disease, and 260 nurses had died from the infection.

A typical example of how the disease spreads from patients to health care workers could be found at a hospital in Solano County, California. A patient entered the emergency room on February 15 displaying severe flu-like symptoms. The patient was admitted. During the four days in the hospital, numerous physicians, nurses, and other staff members interacted with the patient. Eventually, the patient was diagnosed with COVID-19, as were three hospital staff members who had treated the patient.

A Lack of Testing Slows Prevention

One area in which American hospitals found themselves unprepared for treating COVID-19 patients was the lack of available test kits. A test for the disease requires a nurse to insert a 6-inch-long (15 cm) cotton swab deep into the nostril of a patient. The swabs are sent to labs for analysis.

Testing enables doctors to determine who is infected before they show symptoms. Ideally, patients would be quarantined early in their infections, minimizing the chances of spreading the disease to others. But from the earliest days of the pandemic, hospitals faced an insufficient number of test kits.

In March 2020, sixty-one-year-old Michael Campbell developed a cough and a 102°F fever. A resident of the suburban Philadelphia community of Glenside, he suspected he had contracted COVID-19. Yet when he called his local public health department, he was told no test kits were available. Campbell made some calls and found tests available at a hospital in Wilmington, Delaware—a 46-mile (74 km) drive from his home. He made the drive, received the test, and a few days later learned he had tested positive. Later, he learned that others with whom he had contact before he got the test also contracted the disease. He said, "When I got the positive result back I was almost starting to cry because I like to be part of history, but a good history, not this kind of history. I feel so bad that other people have gotten it from me."

Quoted in Ellie Silverman, "Unable to Get Tested for Coronavirus in Pennsylvania, He Drove to Delaware: The Risks and Rewards of 'Test Hopping,'" *Philadelphia Inquirer*, March 30, 2020. www.inquirer.com.

Shortages of Masks and Beds

The Solano County patient was treated before hospital workers were advised to wear masks, plastic face shields, and other protective gear. Once this advice had become widespread, many health care workers had difficulty adhering to safety protocols because protective gear was in short supply. For example, staff members at the nation's 170 hospitals and twelve hundred outpatient clinics administered by the US Department of Veterans Affairs (VA) found severe shortages of protective masks. For weeks, the VA told its employees to reuse their masks for a week even though the masks were designed to be used once and then thrown away. The health care workers protested. They worried that the masks had become contaminated by the virus over the course of a week's use. In fact, by mid-April, the VA reported that 150 staff members had been infected with COVID-19 and 14 of them had died. Finally, on April 20, the VA found new supplies of masks and advised its workers to discard their old masks after a single day's use.

Masks were not the only pieces of equipment the American health care system lacked as the pandemic progressed. Many hospitals developed severe shortages of beds for COVID-19 patients. To make beds available, the US Army Corps of Engineers was enlisted to create new spaces for patients. Over several weeks during the spring of 2020, the corps converted empty sports arenas, hotel lobbies, concert halls, convention centers, college dormitories, and similar facilities into temporary hospitals. For example, in a matter of weeks the corps converted the sprawling Javits Convention Center in New York City into a twenty-nine-hundred-bed hospital. For each patient, the Army Corps of Engineers created a temporary room that was 10 feet (3m) wide by 10 feet (3 m) long.

Prior to the outbreak, New York City hospitals could accommodate 53,000 patients—but that was before the city became the nation's largest hot spot for the virus. As COVID-19 swept through their city, officials realized that number would not be nearly enough. They predicted they would need beds for at least 140,000 more patients. General Todd Semonite, the chief of the Army Corps of Engineers, said the pandemic presented a unique challenge to his unit. Never before in the history of the armed services, he explained, had the military been asked to build tens of thousands of hospital rooms within a few weeks' time. "We've never done a pandemic capability," he said. "We don't have on the shelf designs on how to modify hotels into COVID centers."[38]

A Lack of Ventilators

Perhaps no shortage affected patient treatment more than the lack of ventilators. The disease causes many people to become short of breath. It infects the lungs, leaving dead cells along the walls of the lungs. Over time, the dead cells build up, shrinking the air passages that enable people to breathe. Since it could take several days or weeks for the disease to leave the body, a

In May 2020 Ford employees inspect a ventilator that was assembled at the Ypsilanti, Michigan, plant. Ford and other automakers converted their factories and shifted employees to producing desperately needed ventilators.

patient having trouble breathing during that period often needs to rely on a mechanical ventilator. When using a ventilator, a plastic tube is placed into a patient's lung. This enables the machine to pump air into the lung to help the patient breathe.

Early in the pandemic, public health officials predicted that as many as nine hundred thousand Americans would need ventilators to survive COVID-19. However, there were only two hundred thousand ventilators available in US hospitals. According to James Dwyer, the chief of emergency medicine at Northern Westchester Hospital in New York City, "Those patients don't get off the ventilator for two weeks or three weeks, so the need for these machines is not only driven by the people who need ventilators but also the amount of time that they require on the ventilators."[39]

To address the shortage of ventilators, many American industries that were not otherwise in the medical equipment business retooled their factories to produce the machines. Among the companies that stepped up were automakers Ford Motor Company and General Motors, which assigned their engineers to quickly design ventilators and produce them at their factories. Workers even combed through their companies' huge inventories of parts to see which parts that ordinarily are used in car engines or auto bodies could be employed in hospital ventilators.

Another corporation that retooled a factory to make ventilators was Tesla, which manufactures electric cars as well as solar panels. Tesla retooled a solar panel factory in Buffalo, New York, to manufacture ventilators. "[The factory] will reopen for ventilator production as soon as humanly possible," said Elon Musk, the CEO of Tesla. "We will do anything in our power to help the citizens of New York."[40]

Lives Were Saved

As hospitals endured high infection rates among their workers, a shortage of beds, masks, ventilators, and other vital equipment, there were, nevertheless, many success stories. There

Soon after the COVID-19 pandemic surfaced, public health officials found that equipping health care workers with plastic face shields was an effective way to protect those workers from becoming infected. But many hospitals lacked the shields. Soon, art schools in America employed their 3-D printers, laser cutters, and personnel to make the shields and donate them to local hospitals.

Pratt Institute of Design, an art school in New York City, assigned workers in its 3-D lab to print the headbands for the shields using bendable plastic filament. At the same time, the university's architecture department employed a laser-cutting device to cut the individual face plates out of large clear plastic sheets. Early in the pandemic, Pratt sent its students home as it transitioned to online classes. Therefore, the facilities at Pratt were standing idle when university administrators elected to utilize them to help local hospitals. Within three weeks in March and April 2020, the Pratt workers produced fifteen thousand headbands and face plates that were distributed free to New York City hospitals. Personnel at the hospitals then assembled the headbands and plates into the shields with simple pop-in connections. "When I learned that there was an effort to fill the gap between manufacturers being able to get [the shields] out to medical facilities and our current situation, I immediately thought about the resources at Pratt," said Joseph Morris, an industrial design professor at the school.

Quoted in Pratt Institute of Design, "Pratt Responds to COVID-19: The Institute Unites to Produce Thousands of Face Shields for Hospitals," April 13, 2020. www.pratt.edu.

were many examples of how, despite the pressures that were put on the American health care system, the system did come through. Yanira Soriano, thirty-six, was thirty-four-weeks pregnant (which is about six weeks shy of full term) when she was admitted to Northwell Hospital in New York City on April 2 with severe COVID-19 symptoms.

She was placed on a ventilator, but doctors feared for the safety of the baby. The decision was made to perform a C-section—a

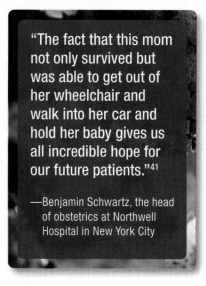

surgical procedure, also known as a cesarean delivery, that enables a doctor to deliver the baby through incisions made in the mother's abdomen and uterus. Delivery by C-section is a common procedure used in as many as a third of all US deliveries. Because a C-section is major surgery, Soriano was placed under general anesthesia for the procedure. In other words, she slept through the birth of her baby.

In fact, she did not meet her new son, Walter, for eleven days—when she finally recovered from COVID-19 and was able to return home. "The fact that this mom not only survived but was able to get out of her wheelchair and walk into her car and hold her baby gives us all incredible hope for our future patients and our existing patients that have COVID disease,"[41] said Benjamin Schwartz, the head of obstetrics at Northwell Hospital.

By early May, the death toll from COVID-19 was staggering: some 69,000 Americans had died from the disease. But more than 1.2 million other Americans had survived, thanks largely to the efforts of health care workers who, often putting their own lives at risk and working with a lack of equipment and supplies, nevertheless found ways to send their patients home fully recovered.

CHAPTER SIX

The Federal Government's Response to COVID-19

On December 31, 2019, the CDC first became aware of reports of a potentially deadly virus afflicting thousands of people in Wuhan, China, a city of about 11 million. CDC officials immediately looked into the reports. Three days later, CDC director Robert Redfield got a phone call from his Chinese counterpart, who confirmed that a dangerous virus was making its way through the city with terrifying speed. He also warned Redfield about the likelihood of the virus spreading to other parts of China and to other countries.

Redfield quickly relayed the news to Alex Azar, the secretary of Health and Human Services (HHS), the agency of the US government that oversees all matters concerning public health. Azar notified the White House's National Security Council (NSC), which assesses foreign threats to America and develops strategies to counter those threats. Once top US government officials were alerted to the danger, they proposed strategies for containing the disease and minimizing its impact on the American people.

But any strategies the CDC and NSC may have developed to address the crisis could not be implemented without the authorization of the president. And in early January 2020, as the nation's top public health officials grew very concerned about the safety of millions of Americans, President Trump was preoccupied with another pressing matter: his impeachment by Congress, and his possible removal from office. "It came up while we were, you know, tied down in the impeachment trial," said Kentucky senator Mitch McConnell, the powerful majority leader of the US Senate. "And I think it diverted the attention of the government, because everything, every day, was all about impeachment."[42]

Impeachment Captivates the Nation

Trump's impeachment had its roots in a July 25, 2019, phone call he placed to the president of Ukraine, Volodymyr Zelensky. During that call, Trump asked Zelensky to investigate Hunter Biden, the son of former vice president Joseph Biden. The elder Biden was by then seeking the nomination as the Democratic candidate for president in the 2020 election. Trump considered Joseph Biden a formidable opponent. Trump's critics believe that he was looking for ways to undermine Biden's candidacy and thought he found what he needed in Hunter Biden's business dealings in Ukraine. Trump has denied this was the case.

Under pressure, the White House released a summary of Trump's phone call with Zelensky. According to that summary, and subsequent testimony by various officials, Trump asked Zelensky to publicly announce an investigation into the activities of Hunter Biden or risk losing $400 million in weapons and other military aid. This assistance was essential to Ukraine's ability to stand up to its hostile larger neighbor, Russia, in border disputes and other issues.

The allegation that Trump had threatened to withhold military aid to an ally to further his personal political fortunes came to the attention of the news media and members of Congress. The US House opened an investigation, gathering testimony from witnesses and other evidence to determine whether the president had abused his powers—an offense that could lead to his impeachment and possible removal from office. The US House of Representatives staged public hearings on its inquiry, which were broadcast live on national television. The hearings, and the evidence that emerged, captivated the nation. On December 13, 2019, the House Judiciary Committee approved two articles of impeachment against the president. It took until January 15, 2020, for the entire House to approve the articles and deliver them to the US Senate. By law, the Senate was then required to hold a trial on the evidence. If, after the conclusion of the trial,

Headlines in the New York Times and other newspapers announce President Donald Trump's impeachment. Trump was preoccupied with the impeachment process even as health officials warned of the coronavirus's spread.

two-thirds of the one hundred members of the Senate voted to convict the president, Trump would be forced out of office.

It was during this chaotic time in Washington, DC, that public health officials became more and more concerned about the growing danger of the new coronavirus. Their efforts to advise Trump of the seriousness of the matter often seemed to fall on deaf ears as the president appeared focused solely on beating back the charges that could ultimately result in his removal from office. The *Washington Post* reported,

> In hindsight, officials said, Azar could have been more forceful in urging Trump to turn at least some of his attention to a threat that would soon pose an even graver test to his presidency, a crisis that would cost American lives and consume the final year of Trump's first term. . . . Azar told several associates that the president believed he was an "alarmist" and Azar struggled to get Trump's attention to focus on the issue.[43]

The trial in the Senate commenced on January 16. It ended February 5 with a vote by the Senate to acquit Trump of the charges. That outcome had been expected given that the Republican Party held a majority of the seats in the Senate. Still, the daily progress of the trial was broadcast live on national television and reported in newspapers while dominating the news and social media. Trump's attention was focused solely on the impeachment trial, as he spent those critical days in January and early February in deep discussions with aides, allies in the Senate, and political commentators. On January 22, Trump was asked by a reporter whether he was concerned about the spread of the virus. "No. Not at all," he responded. "And we have it totally under control."[44]

"We have [the coronavirus] totally under control."[44]

—Donald Trump, the forty-fifth US president

During the COVID-19 pandemic, President Donald Trump often feuded with several of the nation's governors, who begged for a coordinated federal response to help hospitals obtain the equipment and supplies they desperately needed to fight the disease. Many governors called on Trump to invoke his powers under the US Defense Production Act, which enables the president to force US industries to produce supplies that are needed during crises. For example, in late March 2020, New York governor Andrew Cuomo said he was forced into bidding wars with other governors who were attempting to buy medical supplies from the few manufacturers that had them available. "You have manufacturers who sit there and California offers them four dollars, and they say 'well California offered four dollars.' I offer five dollars, another state calls in and offers six dollars. It's not the way to do it."

After receiving a similar complaint from Governor Jay Pritzker of Illinois, Trump lashed out, posting a message on his Twitter account: "Governor of Illinois, and a very small group of certain other Governors . . . shouldn't be blaming the Federal Government for their own shortcomings."

Ultimately, Trump did invoke his powers under the act, but not until early April. Trump ordered companies to manufacture ventilators, nasal swabs, protective gear, and other supplies needed by hospitals.

Quoted in Jeremy Stahl, "Governors Beg for Medical Supplies as Trump Refuses to Act," *Slate,* March 23, 2020. https://slate.com.

Denial and Acknowledgment

On February 5—the day the Senate acquitted Trump of the charges that he misused his presidential powers for personal gain—some ninety-eight hundred citizens in China and other countries had already been infected with the virus. The death toll stood at more than two hundred. The *Diamond Princess* had been quarantined in Japan, and the disease had already started to infect Americans at home.

Although Trump had been preoccupied with the impeachment trial, officials at the CDC and HHS were doing all they could to ensure Americans would be safe. But they hit several roadblocks, with the main obstacle being they had no resources to conduct widespread testing of Americans to determine the extent of the infection. The HHS had no budget to perform millions of tests.

Meanwhile, Trump refused to acknowledge the dangers posed by the coronavirus. On more than one occasion he declared that the United States had the virus "under control." He predicted it would quickly run its course. "It's going to disappear. One day, it's like a miracle, it will disappear," he said at a February 27 news conference. He insisted it posed little risk to most Americans and he accused the Democrats and news media of hyping the story. "The Fake News Media and their partner, the Democrat Party, is doing everything within its semi-considerable power . . . to inflame the CoronaVirus situation,"[45] he tweeted on March 9. Some saw his response as a sign of concern for how a widespread lockdown would damage the economy—and his chances for re-election.

By mid-March, however, the president had publicly acknowledged the severity of the pandemic and began describing himself as being on top of it from the start. "We're using the full power of the federal government to defeat the virus, and that's what we've been doing," Trump said in a March 14 news conference. Three days later, at a March 17 news conference, he declared, "I felt it was a pandemic long before it was called a pandemic."[46]

Appeals for Aid

By mid-February, officials at HHS were making appeals to the White House to free billions of dollars in aid that could be directed toward buying protective masks for health care workers, obtaining ventilators for hospitals, and providing other necessities. Internal squabbling dominated the debate as Trump's closest advisers stood firm. They feared any request for a huge expenditure of money to protect Americans from a deadly pandemic would spark panic. "White House budget hawks argued that appropriating too much money at once when there were only a few US cases would be viewed as alarmist,"[47] the *Washington Post* reported.

Finally, in early March, Trump authorized the submission of a proposal to Congress to provide emergency aid of $2.5 billion to meet the needs of hospitals that expected to be faced with thousands of patients showing life-threatening symptoms. Congress acted on March 6, approving $8 billion, far more than the $2.5 billion the administration had requested. Members of the House and Senate said they looked at the administration's plans and concluded they did not go far enough to protect Americans. Senator Richard Shelby of Alabama explained, "This should not be about politics; this is about doing our job to protect the American people from a potential pandemic. We worked together to craft an aggressive and comprehensive response that provides the resources the experts say they need to combat this crisis."[48]

> "This should not be about politics; this is about doing our job to protect the American people from a potential pandemic."[48]
>
> —Richard Shelby, a senator from Alabama

The body of a COVID-19 victim is unloaded from a refrigerated truck in Brooklyn, New York, before being transferred to a mortuary. Government financial help for struggling individuals and businesses was enacted only after the virus had already swept through America.

By the time the money was appropriated to finance the country's response, COVID-19 had been declared a global pandemic—and it had already swept through America. By the end of March, governors had closed schools and nonessential businesses and ordered citizens to stay home. Social distancing rules were set in place. Sporting events were canceled. Shopping malls closed down. News broadcasts showed the once-bustling streets in America's biggest cities now virtually deserted. Millions of people lost their jobs.

Criticism and Praise

Not surprisingly, Trump's actions in the face of the pandemic brought out many of his fiercest critics. One of them was Biden, who, by April, had virtually sewn up the nomination of the Democratic Party to face Trump in the fall election. "Coronavirus is not Donald Trump's fault," Biden said. "But he does bear responsibility for our response and [not] taking his duties seriously. His failings and his delays [are] causing real pain for so many Americans."[49]

Also not surprising was praise from the president's most devoted supporters. In early May 2020 Missouri governor Mike Parson said, "When you think about where we were at 60 days ago—to do what [Trump] did to get that [aid] package out as early as they did, to almost retool the manufacturing across the United States to make PPE (personal protective equipment) supply for every state. To be critical of that being done and the federal government to get all that done in 60 days, I mean, people just need to sit back and take a breath here and realize what's been accomplished in 60 days by the president."[50]

Historians will one day take a longer look at the devastation that resulted from the COVID-19 pandemic. They will parse the government response to this national and global tragedy. They will analyze the actions of elected officeholders, their advisers, and the agencies that are central to a functioning government. And someday they will try to understand whether the government response was exactly what was needed or whether it was too little, too late.

Emerging from the Pandemic

Nebraska was one of eight states that elected not to issue stay-at-home orders, yet citizens of those states were advised to take precautions when shopping and doing other errands. In early April 2020, Katie Berger visited a local hair salon in her northeastern Nebraska community. A few days later, Berger received a text from the salon owner, advising her that one of the stylists had tested positive for COVID-19. Berger immediately knew what this meant: she could very well have contracted the disease from the infected stylist.

After a few more days, Berger received a call from her state health department advising her officially that she had come into contact with a COVID-19 patient. Even though Berger was not showing symptoms, she was instructed to stay home and self-quarantine. "They said, 'We're calling to inform you that you were exposed to a COVID-19 patient,'" Berger recalled. "It was still pretty scary getting that call, even though I knew it was coming."[51]

The Nebraska Health Department worker who called Berger was taking part in a program known as contact tracing. States across America (and nations around the world) have instituted the program as a method of cutting down on the rate of infection from COVID-19. Essentially, health department officials collect data from

"They said, 'We're calling to inform you that you were exposed to a COVID-19 patient.'"[51]

—Katie Berger, who was exposed to a COVID-19 patient at a Nebraska hair salon

hospitals on who has been infected with the disease. Once they have this information, the health department workers do some detective work—finding out from the patient whom he or she may have come into close contact with during the past few weeks. As they compile a list of names, the contact tracers reach out to those persons to advise them that they may be infected themselves and to self-quarantine for at least two weeks. "The whole point of this process is to make sure that people who have the virus are separated from those who don't," explained Josh Michaud, the associate director for global health policy at the Kaiser Family Foundation, a California organization that studies health care issues. "That includes the original case, who's isolating, and the contacts who might be incubating the disease. If you get them to self-quarantine before they are infectious, then you've essentially stopped the transmis-

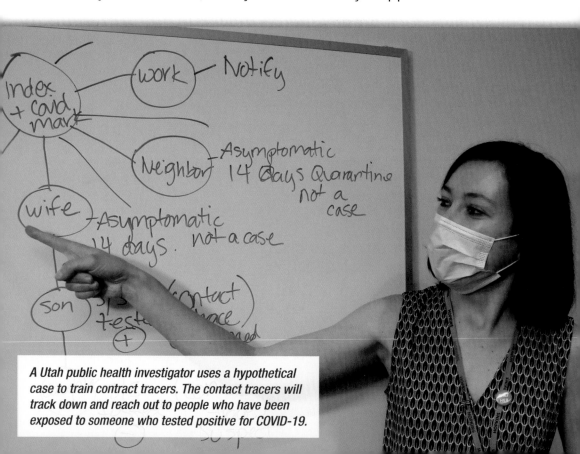

A Utah public health investigator uses a hypothetical case to train contract tracers. The contact tracers will track down and reach out to people who have been exposed to someone who tested positive for COVID-19.

sion of that disease from that transmission train. If you do that with enough contacts, then you've effectively interrupted community transmission."[52]

Contact tracing can be a formidable task. It requires teams of tracers to work the phones or go door-to-door to make personal contacts with individuals to let them know they should self-quarantine. By late April, many state health departments were recruiting workers to pursue contact tracing assignments. By then, the state of Washington had already recruited or reassigned six hundred state employees to work on contact tracing assignments, with plans to hire another nine hundred workers by mid-May. "We want to make sure we can get a hold of every contact and case within 24 hours of that report and get the contacts with them within 24 hours," said John Wiesman, the state's secretary of health. "We're doing some planning now as a system to make sure we could do contact tracing and case interviews for at least 1,000 cases a day if we had to."[53]

> "The whole point of this process is to make sure that people who have the virus are separated from those who don't."[52]
>
> —Josh Michaud, the associate director for global health policy at the Kaiser Family Foundation

Smartphone Applications

As state governments and foreign countries ramped up their contact tracing programs, a number of technology firms were developing apps to aid the efforts. Among those companies were Apple, Microsoft, and Google, which assigned engineers to develop smartphone apps that would help alert a user if he or she encountered a COVID-19 patient while shopping in a grocery store or perhaps after sharing a park bench with the patient.

If someone suspected they had contracted the disease, they could enter the data into the app on their phones. The phone would then send a signal to other app users, alerting them they may have been in contact with a COVID-19 patient. During those previous weeks, the apps would have been recording the data drawn from nearby contacts. The app would then know whom to contact in case the user started showing symptoms. The infected person may have been in close contact with the app user for only a few seconds, but, nevertheless, the app would identify the user as potentially being infected. By late April 2020, the first apps had entered the test phase.

British health officials enthusiastically endorsed the use of apps, urging people to download and install them as soon as they were available. British health secretary Matthew Hancock explained, "If you become unwell with the symptoms of coronavirus, you can securely tell this new . . . app and the app will then send an alert anonymously to other app users that you've been in significant contact with over the past few days, even before you had symptoms, so that they know and can act accordingly."[54]

But there was some pushback against using the apps. Critics wondered whether governments could use the data as a method of keeping track of citizens' whereabouts. This was a concern both in democratic societies, where people generally move about freely, and in countries with authoritarian leaders, who may wish to silence dissidents. More than three hundred scientists and engineers from twenty-five countries in Europe signed a letter protesting the use of contact tracing apps. In the letter, they asserted, "We are concerned that some 'solutions' to the crisis may . . . result in systems which would allow unprecedented surveillance of society at large."[55]

Treatments and Vaccines

As government health officials ramped up their contact tracing efforts, physicians and scientists across the world worked hard to develop both a treatment and a vaccine. Testing for both had already started by the spring of 2020. A treatment would reduce the virus's effects before they became life-threatening. A vaccine helps gain immunity to the disease much like flu vaccines do for outbreaks of influenza.

While other countries instructed citizens to stay home during the COVID-19 pandemic, that strategy was not pursued in Sweden, where restaurants, schools, stores, and offices all remained open. Sweden elected to practice herd immunity. In other words, people were encouraged to interact with others under the theory that a majority of people contracting the disease would either show no symptoms or be mildly affected and recover quickly. They would then be immune from contracting the disease again. If enough people are immune to the disease, says Jaquelin Dudley, a professor of infectious diseases at the University of Texas at Austin, it will not spread widely through the population. Therefore, the likelihood that others who are susceptible to the disease would be infected is low.

By May 2020, experts were not prepared to declare herd immunity a successful strategy. By then, Sweden—with a national population of more than 10 million people—had suffered some 2,800 deaths due to COVID-19. Moreover, elderly patients accounted for 86 percent of the deaths, meaning the country did not do a good job of protecting people with weak immune systems. As Craig Janes, the director of the School of Public Health at the University of Waterloo in Canada, explained, "They do have a lot of cases and they are seeing a fairly significant amount of mortality, particularly, as we do here, in long-term care facilities, retirement homes. So I'm not sure that, when it's the end of the day, it will be highlighted as a successful approach."

Quoted in Hannah Jackson, "Sweden Took a Softer COVID-19 Approach. Has It Been Effective?," Global News, May 4, 2020. https://globalnews.ca.

New drugs that either treat or provide immunity from a disease ordinarily take many years to develop. In the United States, the drugs need to be synthesized in a lab, meaning scientists have to find the right combinations of chemicals or biological substances that make them work. Tests are often first conducted on animals and then, in clinical trials, on people. Clinical trials often take many months—and sometimes more than a year. The US Food and Drug Administration (FDA) closely monitors the trials and does not approve the drug for widespread use until the agency is satisfied it is both safe and effective. The entire process, from initial development to approval, can easily take twelve years.

With the pandemic's spread, however, the FDA said it would fast-track approval for new drugs that are shown to treat COVID-19 and provide immunity through vaccinations. Several US and foreign pharmaceutical companies quickly poured their resources into developing such drugs. Still, executives in the American pharmaceutical industry predicted a vaccine for COVID-19 would not be available until at least 2021. One joint venture paired John-

Antibodies and COVID-19

Antibodies are central to three avenues of research being pursued in the quest to shut down COVID-19. Antibodies can help identify people who were infected with the coronavirus (which causes the disease) and might now be immune. It is also possible that infusions of coronavirus antibodies (administered by injection) will block the virus and prevent or reduce infection. A third avenue of research involves a vaccine that will enable the body to make its own protective antibodies before a person is exposed to the virus. Researchers pursuing these and other ways of fighting COVID-19 know that the human immune system makes white blood cells. These cells produce Y-shaped molecules called antibodies. Antibodies can keep viruses from infecting the cells. But that protection may depend on where the antibody grips the virus and how tightly it holds on.

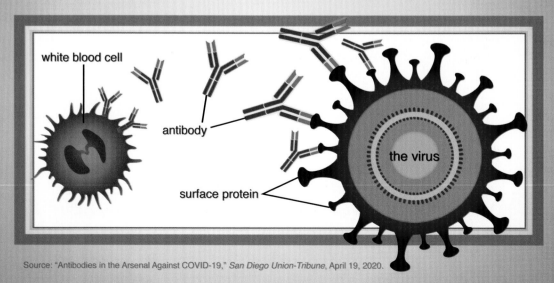

Source: "Antibodies in the Arsenal Against COVID-19," *San Diego Union-Tribune*, April 19, 2020.

son & Johnson, a major American pharmaceutical producer, with a federal agency, the US Biomedical Advanced Research and Development Authority. Executives at Johnson & Johnson said the company and the federal agency planned to spend a total of $1 billion between them in this joint venture to develop a COVID-19 vaccine and make it available—at no cost to patients—at some point in 2021. "The world is facing an urgent public health crisis and we are committed to doing our part to make a COVID-19 vaccine available and affordable globally as quickly as possible,"[56] said Johnson & Johnson CEO Alex Gorsky.

> "The world is facing an urgent public health crisis and we are committed to doing our part to make a COVID-19 vaccine available and affordable globally as quickly as possible."[56]
>
> —Alex Gorsky, the CEO of Johnson & Johnson

The Best Hope for the Future

As for a drug to treat the symptoms of COVID-19, a federal agency, the National Institutes of Health (NIH), said it would partner with sixteen pharmaceutical companies. The companies agreed to share research data in order to develop an effective treatment. "We need to have all hands on deck from every sector to speed up the process of identifying those treatments that are going to work and . . . make sure they're safe and effective in the maximum possible speed,"[57] said Francis Collins, director of the NIH.

By the spring of 2020, several drugs were already under development. One of these drugs, known as remdesivir, was already in human trials after tests on monkeys showed positive results. Nevertheless, due to the trials that needed to be performed as well as the amount of time needed to produce millions of doses of an effective drug, it was expected that drugs capable of treating COVID-19 would not be available until 2021.

Although pandemics have swept through human culture before, none of them moved as swiftly as COVID-19. Emerging from a wet market in the Chinese city of Wuhan in late 2019, it took just weeks before the pandemic posed an international threat to millions of people.

Unlike the pandemics of the past—the Spanish flu or the Black Death—the COVID-19 pandemic traveled across the world during an era in which medicine had evolved into a highly developed science equipped with tools capable of conquering the disease. As COVID-19 dominated life in 2020, the best hope for the future rested on the efforts of the scientists and physicians who sought the treatments and vaccines for the disease.

Introduction: A Danger to All

1. Quoted in Kat Russell, "Tiffin Teen Recovers from 'Unbearable' Coronavirus," *Cedar Rapids Gazette*, April 13, 2020. www.thegazette.com.
2. Quoted in Nicole Pelletiere, "Healthy 18-Year-Old Speaks Out After Contracting COVID-19: 'It Can Happen to Anyone,'" *Good Morning America*, April 6, 2020. www.goodmorningamerica.com.
3. Quoted in Al Jazeera, "Pandemic: WHO Declares Coronavirus a Major Global Threat," March 11, 2020. www.aljazeera.com.
4. Quoted in Russell, "Tiffin Teen Recovers from 'Unbearable' Coronavirus."

Chapter One: The Pandemic Spreads Across the Globe

5. Jason Beaubien, "Why They're Called 'Wet Markets'—and What Health Risks They Might Pose," *Goats and Soda* (blog), NPR, January 31, 2020. www.npr.org.
6. Quoted in Ollie Williams, "There Will Be More 'Zoonotic' Viruses Where COVID Came From," *Forbes*, April 22, 2020. www.forbes.com.
7. Victor Davis Hanson, "Coronavirus Crisis: It's What We Don't Know That Scares Us," Fox News, March 5, 2020. www.foxnews.com.
8. Quoted in Alex Ward, "How Spain's Coronavirus Outbreak Got So Bad So Fast—and How Spaniards Are Trying to Cope," Vox, March 20, 2020. www.vox.com.
9. Quoted in Elizabeth Chuck, "American on Coronavirus Lockdown in Italy: 'It's Surreal. It's Dystopian,'" NBC News, March 11, 2020. www.nbcnews.com.
10. Quoted in Chuck, "American on Coronavirus Lockdown in Italy."

Chapter Two: Life Under the Lockdown

11. Quoted in Sam McManis, "The Dash to Aisle 11 for Precious Toilet Paper amid Flagstaff's Coronavirus Response," *Arizona Daily Sun*, March 29, 2020. https://azdailysun.com.
12. Quoted in Ari Altstedter and Jinshan Hong, "Why People Are Panic Buying as Coronavirus Spreads," *Time*, March 10, 2020. https://time.com.
13. Quoted in Lauren Zumbach, "Rationing of High-Demand Goods, Shoppers in Masks and Reminders to Keep Your Distance. This Is the Brave New World of Pandemic Shopping," *Chicago Tribune*, March 31, 2020. www.chicagotribune.com.
14. Quoted in Jeff Preval, "Instacart Continues to Fill Orders, amid Talks of Strike," WGRZ, March 30, 2020. www.wgrz.com.
15. Quoted in Cristina Rendon, "How Nextdoor Is Inspiring Neighbors Helping Neighbors in a Time of Crisis," KTVU, March 19, 2020. www.ktvu.com.
16. Quoted in Fox 29, "NJ Boy Commended for Asking for Food Donations Instead of Birthday Gifts," April 18, 2020. www.fox29.com.
17. Quoted in Alfred Lubrano, "How Kids Cope," *Philadelphia Inquirer*, April 29, 2020, p. C2.
18. Quoted in Manny Fernandez, "Conservatives Fuel Protests Against Coronavirus Lockdowns," *New York Times*, April 18, 2020. www.nytimes.com.

Chapter Three: Struggling Workers and Businesses

19. Quoted in Emmie Martin, "This Couple Was Making $56,000 and Had Paid Off $125,000 in Debt—Then They Both Lost Their Jobs in the Coronavirus Pandemic," CNBC, April 1, 2020. www.cnbc.com.
20. Quoted in Nelson D. Schwartz, "'Nowhere to Hide' as Unemployment Permeates the Economy," *New York Times*, April 16, 2020. www.nytimes.com.
21. Quoted in Michael Sainato, "'We're Risking Our Life': Coronavirus Takes a Toll on Essential Workers Still on the Job," *The Guardian* (Manchester, UK), April 12, 2020. www.theguardian.com.
22. Quoted in Caitlin Dickerson and Miriam Jordan, "South Dakota Meat Plant Is Now Country's Biggest Coronavirus Hot Spot," *New York Times*, April 16, 2020. www.nytimes.com.

23. Quoted in Amy S. Rosenberg, "Laid Off by Shore Casinos, They Wait in Line for Food," *Philadelphia Inquirer*, April 23, 2020, p. B1.

24. Quoted in Anna Bahney, "She Got Her Stimulus Payment. Here's How She Plans to Use It," CNN, April 15, 2020. www .cnn.com.

25. Quoted in Angela Wilson, "Working from Home Has Its Perks, Challenges," *Galveston (TX) Daily News*, April 19, 2020. www.galvnews.com.

Chapter Four: Schools Close Their Doors

26. Quoted in Jazmine Hughes, "All Dressed Up, with No Prom to Go To," *New York Times*, April 17, 2020. www.nytimes.com.

27. Quoted in Hughes, "All Dressed Up, with No Prom to Go To."

28. Quoted in Cory Turner, Diane Adame, and Elissa Nadworny, "'There's a Huge Disparity': What Teaching Looks Like During Coronavirus," NPR, April 11, 2020. www.npr.org.

29. Quoted in Turner, Adame, and Nadworny, "'There's a Huge Disparity.'"

30. Quoted in *New York Times*, "Teachers and Students Describe a Remote-Learning Life," April 24, 2020, p. L4.

31. Quoted in *New York Times*, "Teachers and Students Describe a Remote-Learning Life," p. L4.

32. Quoted in Howard Blume and Sonali Kohli, "15,000 L.A. High School Students are AWOL Online, 40,000 Fail to Check in Daily amid Coronavirus Closures," *Los Angeles Times*, March 30, 2020. www.latimes.com.

33. Quoted in Dana Goldstein, Adam Popescu, and Nikole Hannah-Jones, "As School Moves Online, Many Students Stay Logged Out," *New York Times*, April 8, 2020. www.nytimes .com.

34. Quoted in Erin Mansfield and Shelly Conlon, "Coronavirus for Kids Without Internet: Quarantined Worksheets, Learning in Parking Lots," *USA Today*, April 4, 2020. www.usatoday.com.

35. Quoted in Elissa Nadworny, "With Schools Closed, Kids with Disabilities Are More Vulnerable than Ever," *All Things Considered,* NPR, March 27, 2020. www.npr.org.

36. Quoted in Nadworny, "With Schools Closed, Kids with Disabilities Are More Vulnerable than Ever."

Chapter Five: Hospitals and Health Care Workers Fight the Pandemic

37. Quoted in Michael Rothfeld, Jesse Drucker, and William K. Rashbaum, "The Heartbreaking Last Texts of a Hospital Worker on the Front Lines," *New York Times*, April 15, 2020. www.nytimes.com.
38. Quoted in Bryan Llenas and Lucas Tomlinson, "Race to Build Temporary Hospitals Nationwide as Coronavirus Spreads," Fox News, March 27, 2020. www.foxnews.com.
39. Quoted in Jackie Salo, "Coronavirus: What Is a Ventilator and Why Is There a Shortage?," *New York Post*, April 1, 2020. https://nypost.com.
40. Quoted in Timothy B. Lee, "Tesla Plans to Retool Solar Panel Factory to Make Medtronic Ventilators," Ars Technica, March 26, 2020. https://arstechnica.com.
41. Quoted in Rachel DeSantis, "Mom Meets Baby for First Time After Surviving Coronavirus: 'An Incredibly Proud Moment,'" People, Microsoft News, April 16, 2020. www.msn.com.

Chapter Six: The Federal Government's Response to COVID-19

42. Quoted in Felicia Sonmez, "McConnell Claims Impeachment 'Diverted the Attention' of Trump Administration from Coronavirus Response," *Washington Post*, March 30, 2020. www.washingtonpost.com.
43. Yasmeen Abutaleb et al., "The US Was Beset by Denial and Dysfunction as the Coronavirus Raged," *Washington Post*, April 4, 2020. www.washingtonpost.com.
44. Quoted in Abutaleb et al., "The US Was Beset by Denial and Dysfunction as the Coronavirus Raged."
45. Quoted in Harry Stevens and Shelly Tan, "From 'It's Going to Disappear' to 'WE WILL WIN THIS WAR,' How the President's Response to the Coronavirus Has Changed Since January," *Washington Post*, March 31, 2020. www.washingtonpost.com.
46. Quoted in Harry Stevens and Shelly Tan, "From 'It's Going to Disappear' to 'WE WILL WIN THIS WAR.'"
47. Abutaleb et al., "The US Was Beset by Denial and Dysfunction as the Coronavirus Raged."

48. Quoted in Alan He and Grace Segers, "House Passes $8.3 Billion Package in Emergency Funding to Fight Coronavirus Outbreak," CBS News, March 4, 2020. www.cbsnews.com.

49. Quoted in Seema Mehta, "Joe Biden Blasts Trump's Response to Coronavirus Day After Their Phone Call," *Los Angeles Times*, April 20, 2020. www.latimes.com.

50. Quoted in Sam Dorman, "Missouri Governor Praises Trump Admin's COVID-19 Response: 'Almost Moved Mountains,'" Fox News, May 16, 2020, www.foxnews.com.

Chapter Seven: Emerging from the Pandemic

51. Quoted in Selena Simmons-Duffin, "How Contact Tracing Works and How It Can Help Reopen the Country," NPR, April 14, 2020. www.npr.org.

52. Quoted in Simmons-Duffin, "How Contact Tracing Works and How It Can Help Reopen the Country."

53. Quoted in Arielle Dreher, "More Testing, Contact Tracing, Supplies Needed Before State Dials Back Social Distancing," *Spokane (WA) Spokesman-Review*, April 19, 2020. www.spokesman.com.

54. Quoted in Laurie Clarke, "How Will the NHS COVID-19 Contact-Tracing App Work and When Will It Go Live?," *New Statesman*, April 2, 2020. https://tech.newstatesman.com.

55. Quoted in Reuters, "European Scientists and Researchers Raise Privacy Concerns over Coronavirus Tracing Apps," VentureBeat, April 21, 2020. https://venturebeat.com.

56. Quoted in "Johnson & Johnson Announces a Lead Vaccine Candidate for COVID-19; Landmark New Partnership with U.S. Department of Health & Human Services; and Commitment to Supply One Billion Vaccines Worldwide for Emergency Pandemic Use," Johnson & Johnson, March 30, 2020. www.jnj.com.

57. Quoted in Maureen Pao, "NIH Launches Effort to Speed Up Development of COVID-19 Treatments," *All Things Considered,* NPR, April 17, 2020. www.npr.org.

Center for Infectious Disease Research and Policy (CIDRAP)—www.cidrap.umn.edu

Maintained by the University of Minnesota, CIDRAP has made several resources available about COVID-19. Visitors to the group's website can find maps charting the spread of the disease; a timeline reporting how the disease emerged from Wuhan, China; and a video showing how the disease spread, county by county, in America.

Johns Hopkins Center for Health Security
www.centerforhealthsecurity.org

The center examines pandemics and other international health threats. By accessing the link for "Medical and Public Health Preparedness and Response," visitors can download copies of the organization's report *A National Plan to Enable Comprehensive COVID-19 Case Finding and Contact Tracing in the US.*

Mayo Clinic—www.mayoclinic.org

The renowned medical center based in Rochester, Minnesota, maintains a website that is following the development of vaccines for COVID-19. It discusses the different types of vaccines under development as well as the expected timeline that must unfold before they can be made available to the public.

Mütter Museum—http://muttermuseum.org

Maintained by the College of Physicians of Philadelphia, the Mütter Museum features exhibits on past pandemics that have afflicted the world. Visitors to the museum's website can find a story and photographs behind the museum's exhibit *Spit Spreads Death: The Influenza Pandemic of 1918–19 in Philadelphia*.

US Centers for Disease Control and Prevention (CDC)
www.cdc.gov

The CDC is the federal government's chief agency that monitors the spread of COVID-19 and develops strategies to stem the spread of the infection. By accessing the "COVID-19" tab on the CDC website, visitors can learn about symptoms of the disease, how tests are administered, and precautions to take when venturing outside the home.

World Health Organization (WHO)—www.who.int

An agency of the United Nations, WHO monitors international threats to human health. By accessing the "COVID-19 Situation Dashboard" on the WHO website, visitors can find a map showing how the disease has crossed the world as well as statistics on the number of cases, which is updated daily.

Books

Catherine Arnold, *Pandemic 1918: Eyewitness Accounts from the Greatest Medical Holocaust in Modern History*. New York: St. Martin's Griffin, 2020.

Catherine Carver, *Immune: How Your Body Defends and Protects You*. New York: Bloomsbury, Sigma, 2017.

Daniel Defoe, *Illustrated Journal of the Plague Year: 300th Anniversary Edition*. Orina, CA: SeaWolf, 2020.

Michael T. Osterholm and Mark Olshaker, *Deadliest Enemy: Our War Against Killer Germs*. New York: Little, Brown, 2017.

Frank M. Snowden, *Epidemics and Society: From the Black Death to the Present*. New Haven, CT: Yale University Press, 2020.

Steffanie Strathdee, Thomas Patterson, and Teresa Barker, *The Perfect Predator: A Scientist's Race to Save Her Husband from a Deadly Superbug*. New York: Hachette, 2019.

Internet Sources

Ari Altstedter and Jinshan Hong, "Why People Are Panic Buying as Coronavirus Spreads," *Time*, March 10, 2020. https://time.com.

Jason Beaubien, "Why They're Called 'Wet Markets'—and What Health Risks They Might Pose," *Goats and Soda* (blog), NPR, January 31, 2020. www.npr.org.

Jazmine Hughes, "All Dressed Up, with No Prom to Go To," *New York Times*, April 17, 2020. www.nytimes.com.

Nicole Pelletiere, "Healthy 18-Year-Old Speaks Out After Contracting COVID-19: 'It Can Happen to Anyone,'" *Good Morning America,* April 6, 2020. www.goodmorningamerica.com.

Michael Sainato, "'We're Risking Our Life': Coronavirus Takes a Toll on Essential Workers Still on the Job," *The Guardian* (Manchester, UK), April 12, 2020. www.theguardian.com.

PICTURE CREDITS

ABOUT THE AUTHOR

Hal Marcovitz is a former newspaper reporter and columnist who has written more than two hundred books for young readers. His daughter, Ashley Marcovitz, is the manager of the 3-D printing lab at Pratt Institute of Design in New York City. Ashley was among the Pratt employees who were called back to their jobs during the COVID-19 pandemic to help make fifteen thousand protective face plates for New York City hospital workers.